Global Leadership Ltd UK

The

Heathrow

Report 2015

“What the Airports Commission Missed”

Gordan Glass

The Transport Safety Organisation

First published in the United Kingdom in 2014

By Global Leadership Ltd, UK

www.GlobalLeadershipLtd.com

ISBN 978-1-910268-01-8

Written with the assistance of
Jennifer Manson

The Small Print

In providing this content, the author is acting in the manner and role of an investigative journalist and whistleblower, in that he is bringing information and alternative viewpoints into public awareness with the intention of increasing the range of understanding of the reader in the wider public interest.

The author believes the content to be true, but makes no warranty, claim, proposition or suggestion that it is: it is presented as the author's personal opinion only and readers are asked to judge for themselves the limits of their own agreement with the content and to recognize their conclusions as their own subjective judgments. Neither the publisher nor the author shall be held liable for any errors, offence, harm, loss or any other damages, however caused, resulting from the use of this report or its contents: caveat lector.

Furthermore, the information provided within must not be relied upon as being up to date and must not be relied upon as legal or professional advice, nor as a substitute for such, as different professionals may have different opinions on the content.

All links provided are for information and reference only and no warranty is provided or implied regarding the content or accuracy of any related material.

DEDICATION

To the many people of London who live under the Heathrow flight paths

with the resultant constant disruption to their lives and with the insidious fear of an aircraft crash

in the mistaken belief that some organisation is looking after the risks to their health and safety

Table of Contents

FOREWORD 1

INTRODUCTION 3

A quick policy-making quiz/On Approach 9

1 A Failure of Democracy 13

2 Overview 19

3 About the Author 29

4 A Short History of Heathrow and Policy 35

5 The Need for Transformation 47

6 A Different Approach is Needed 55

7 No Third Runway 65

8 Problems with the Focus on Heathrow 69

9 The Heathrow Myths 99

10 Conclusion & Transport Safety Commission 109

11 Extracts from the Terminal 5 Inquiry Report 117

12 RECOMMENDATIONS 123

FOREWORD

Awaiting Submission

INTRODUCTION

The Transport Safety Organisation

The Transport Safety Organisation was established as a Private Company Limited by Guarantee in October 1999 after the Ladbroke Grove rail crash that month (in which 31 people died) and after the end of the Heathrow Terminal 5 Planning Inquiry that year, when it became clear that the UK was lacking an organisation with a mandate and responsibility to focus on the health and safety of the public adversely affected – or potentially affected – by transport operations (particularly air, rail and ferry transport; the typical field of major public disasters).

The company has never traded, in terms of financial activity. It has operated in name only to bring greater public and institutional awareness of the absence of a designated public institution in the UK with clear responsibility for care for the health and safety of the wider public beyond the limited current focus on passengers travelling within transport vehicles.

In transport infrastructure planning in the UK, it is notable that public and societal risk is not normally a factor properly considered before decisions are made on the location of public transport facilities.

The lack of public resources and attention to this field has meant that the Transport Safety Organisation has necessarily had limited reach over the last decade and a half; however the dire need for such an organisation remains, particularly as the current approach to corporate responsibility and societal risk means that no one is responsible or liable for the sometimes serious societal risk associated with transport operations.

To the UK Airports Commission

This report to the UK Airports Commission, chaired by Howard Davies, draws attention to the continuing absence of proper institutional focus on the wider societal risks of transport operation, both generally and specifically in relation to the operation of Heathrow Airport.

The risk of an aircraft crash on London remains around one every ten years. In 1998, at the Terminal 5 Inquiry, the range was established by the author of this report – who was the only body to oppose the development on the grounds of the crash risk to London – to be between 5-14 years. This probability range was derived from crash statistics presented by a witness for the Government. This risk was considered unacceptable at the time of the inquiry. Yet Heathrow operations have continued to develop over the years, with the risk increasing correspondingly, as the Inspector highlighted in his Report that they would.

The lives of a very large number of people around airports are seriously disrupted by the well-established adverse health consequences of noise and pollution from aircraft activity. Yet the UK Government bodies and the industry continue to maintain a complex system specifically designed to misrepresent both the impact and the risks associated with air transport, in the knowledge that the public are specifically barred from challenging this system in the UK courts.

Through the conclusions in its Interim Report on the development of Heathrow, the Airports Commission has demonstrated an apparent lack of understanding of many of the serious issues involved.

The appointment of a Commission with an apparent mandate, imposed by the Government, to continue to focus on a Heathrow "hub" and pursue more growth in the industry is yet another mechanism to remove the public from involvement in the decision-making.

The Need for Public Authorities

Because of the lack of resources for the Transport Safety Organisation, this report can only provide a limited overview of the problems. Although this report is based upon detailed analyses of the necessary data, resources do not permit the provision of evidential data and analysis in this report. Such analysis, together with the necessary challenge to Government and industry interpretation of complex data is sufficiently important to society to require the provision of proper publicly funded and mandated Transport Health and Safety Authorities, to which the public have rights of access and appeal in law.

This report is not designed to be an academic report, but to draw the attention of the Commission and the public, from an overview, to matters that appear to have been overlooked. In particular, it is designed to encourage public discussion on a subject that is generally kept hidden from public view, especially in the case of societal risk.

The report is written in the hope that the Commission will pursue the recommendations herein and work to protect people harmed by or at risk from air transport industry operations, rather than compound the failures of previous decision-makers who have, in many cases, merely supported fallacious, one-sided, and self-interested industry arguments.

Unfortunately the Commission's interim report reads as though it were written by the industry – which it may well have been – as a self-serving justification for the growth of the industry, regardless of the very serious adverse consequences.

The Commission has been charged to provide an evidential basis for its decision-making, yet it appears to have focused its report almost entirely on the traditionally flawed economic assumptions and methodology provided by the industry and the Government. In its report, it clearly dismisses the contrary evidence of public harm with only a few scattered paragraphs of reference, and very little action in response.

A QUICK POLICY-MAKING QUIZ

QUESTION 1: When will public risk policy change?

ANSWER: (a) When someone reports that the statistical chance of a crash on London is about one in every 10years?

(b) When an aircraft crashes on London?

(c) When three aircraft have crashed on London?

The first should cause action to prevent the crashes,

but it has not – yet.

QUESTION 2: Which noise exposure matters more?

ANSWER: (a) Average noise level increases 1dB over London?

(b) A young mother is prevented from sleeping night and day?

(c) A father crashes his car because of sleep deprivation?

(d) Teaching has to stop in schools every minute?

QUESTION 3: How are policy decisions made – from theory or from reality?

ANSWER: From theoretical calculations

ON APPROACH

This is what a jumbo jet looks like

When it is coming towards you at dusk

One every minute or so…

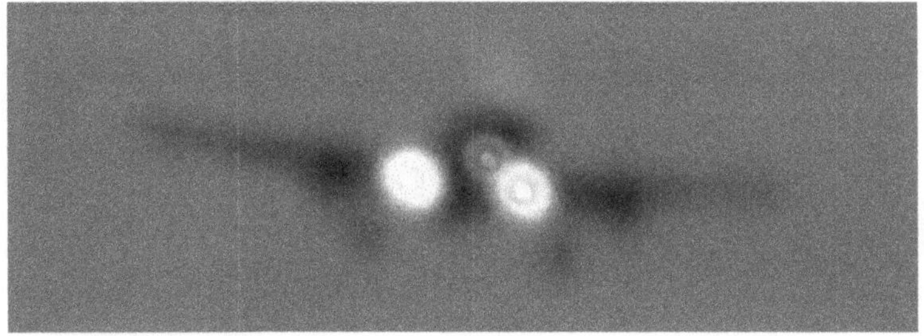

Chapter 1

A Failure of Democracy: No voice for the people in the UK

The material in this book is not new. Very many people, over very many decades, have expressed the concerns within this report. These concerns are based upon sound detailed technical evidence and long experience.

Yet neither the air transport industry nor the government regulatory bodies associated with the sector want to hear these concerns. They are rather like the proverbial three monkeys with their hands over their ears, eyes and mouth: Hear nothing; See nothing; Say nothing.

The passenger numbers through Heathrow Airport continue to escalate alarmingly – beyond public control – along with the consequential public health and safety risks, because most aircraft to Heathrow approach low over central London, even the Houses of Parliament. Parliamentarians and Local Authorities around Heathrow know of these problems from their constituents and have known of them for decades. Yet they have been powerless to influence the faceless civil servants who advise their ministers. Why? Because, as in so many other industries, the democratic process has been hijacked by the continuous stream of self-serving information provided by the businesses in the sector.

For reasons which it does not reveal, the UK Government doesn't want to listen to people who are harmed by its decisions. It seems still to be living on the outdated Victorian principle that "children should be seen and not heard" and even better, ignored. For many decades, the people living around Heathrow and other major UK airports – and their elected representatives – have taken every democratic opportunity to get their concerns heard. Yet they have continued to be ignored and sidelined. Why?

Government decision-making processes do not involve every interested party sitting around a table trying to find a sensible solution; they involve the old model of decisions made in private, by a few people with their own agenda, imposing solutions on everyone else. People who are harmed by these decisions are left having to object to proposals and decisions in order to try to remedy the harm, but without any democratic means for doing so.

Public consultation processes deliberately exclude seeking the views of people who are affected by any particular activity: specifically to avoid "skewing the data". Such consultation processes therefore actually do, deliberately, "skew the data" – in an often blatantly fraudulent manner – by asking questions that elicit the response required by the industry.

A lucrative business can spend money – huge sums – on marketing its case to persuade civil servants and ministers that their solution is the best one. However, in doing so, they naturally avoid presenting the opposing case with the disadvantages and the harm that their proposed solution will cause. People being harmed or disadvantaged do not get any funding to present their case as effectively or positively as business, so their disadvantage is compounded. This tends to make people angry because they feel disenfranchised and unheard. So they do not trust MPs or the Government.

They are then dismissed even more as “negative, complainers and moaners” because they end up having to argue against the pre-presented “positive” business case, typically for “growth” of the business. The Airports Commission apparently continues to fall into this trap of not wanting to believe or value the opposing arguments.

This is compounded by the Government’s similar preconceptions, in favour of “growth” of the industry, which set the objectives for the Commission. These preconceptions themselves are founded on invalid and outdated assumptions and values.

People disadvantaged by decisions end up having to fight or try to change an unsatisfactory system where nobody is in charge of improving the decision-making process. Again, they are then dismissed as being negative: their human rights dismissed too.

"Objectors" cannot be positive about a proposal that is harmful to them. However businesses can be positive because their solutions will provide them with positive outcomes. So the industry proposals are presented as a positive priority, with people disadvantaged placed into a negative subsidiary position as objectors. They are therefore ignored and sidelined at decision time.

Why do UK Governments – unlike many other governments – continue to operate systems and impose development solutions that unnecessarily place large numbers of the public at considerable risk of harm?

The Government has established systems that deliberately misrepresent levels of harm and risk that arise from industry operations – and has also barred certain actions in the Courts. This gives the

Government the ability to drive through policies that increase the harm and risk to the population, instead of caring for and protecting the population. By what method can these systems be changed? Apparently, none!

The industry runs the Government.

Chapter 2
Overview

2.1 Designing a better future for the UK air transport system

With a focus on Heathrow, this report argues that it is time for transformative change in UK air transport policy.

It is a response to the Airports Commission, chaired by Sir Howard Davies, and aims to raise and broaden the perspective of that Commission in its search for future solutions.

There is common agreement that the air travel industry exists to help people travel around the world and enjoy the freedom, excitement and adventure that travel generates; and it also exists to create profits for business. In other words, there is agreement that air travel is useful to society. However, the downsides are very great, too, and for decades the Government and the industry have swept them under the carpet.

In the public launch of his Interim Report on the 17th December 2013, Sir Howard stated that the final Report "is supposed to make recommendations for maintaining the UK's status as an international aviation hub" and that "the purpose of the Interim Report is to set out the evidence base on which that eventual decision will be made" and "to make a number of recommendations for making the best use of existing capacity in the short to medium term".

It is important to ask whether these objectives of the Commission are consistent with what is actually best for air transport policy in this country, and how these objectives protect the residents around airports from the relentless harm and risk to which they are already being subjected.

In the development of any mission, it is helpful to look not only at the purpose but also at the greater long-term vision one is trying to achieve and the values that would be embodied in the achievement of that vision. What is missing here is an answer to the question:

Why has the Commission been given the objective to "maintain" (and by implication also grow) "the UK's status as an international aviation hub", in the face of the indisputable risks and harm to the population?

2.2 Negative impacts need to be addressed

Development of airports and air transport generates current and potential negative impacts, which need to be addressed, as they can (and do) create real harm to the population affected by the airport operations. In particular, these are:

- **safety and associated societal risk;**
- **health effects such as noise and pollution.**

The primary purpose of this report is to address the misconceptions about how these impacts are being handled, by the Government (in terms of policy), by the air transport industry and also by the current Airports Commission.

The major focus of the Airports Commission's Interim Report has been on the expansion of Heathrow. On the surface this appears to be the easiest way to increase airport capacity, but it can also be seen as another short-term, compromise solution, both for the industry and for the people who live around Heathrow. An important factor to consider is that expansion of Heathrow would inevitably increase the negative consequences for the people who live in the highly-populated areas of Greater London under the flight paths.

2.3 Another hub airport

It is also important to consider in more depth the proposal for another hub, such as that supported by the Mayor of London in the Thames Estuary. This concept gives an obvious, long-term, clearly workable alternative, demonstrated by the fact that Britain built a similar airport at Hong Kong before it was handed over to China. Such an airport location would be unique as the societal risks would be virtually zero.

2.4 Best use of existing capacity

Part of the Airports Commission's objective is "to make a number of recommendations for making the best use of existing capacity in the short to medium term".

By focusing on Heathrow and short-listing two proposals for Heathrow, the Commission has overlooked the fact that Terminal 5 opened in 2008 specifically to provide extra capacity and growth in passenger throughput for the next decade and beyond.

The concept for the planning application for Terminal 5 was to enable the airport to be reconfigured for much larger wide-bodied aircraft, which have now only just started to come on-stream. This consent was indeed designed to "make best use of the existing capacity" of the two runways at Heathrow. This was designed and approved on the basis that BAA stated at the T5 Inquiry that there would be no need for a third runway with T5.

The increase in permitted aircraft numbers, combined with the increasing use of larger aircraft means that Heathrow has hardly begun to use the massive increase in capacity provided by the T5 planning consent. There is therefore no need for more capacity at Heathrow for many years to come.

2.5 The need for effective leadership

There is a chronic need for more effective public sector leadership and strategic planning within the air transport industry, and the Airports Commission was presumably intended to be a step towards providing that leadership.

That being the case, there is also a need to examine the Commission's implicit mandate for growth of the industry and also a need for an improved set of criteria to provide a more accurate evidence-base for decisions.

Above all, there continues to be a dire need for a better and more democratic long-term decision-making process as a whole.

The democratic feedback process from those who are harmed by airport and aircraft operations is currently not working in the way that might be expected or desired. Important components of decision-making, such as public safety and quality of life as a whole, are not taken into account to the same extent as business and financial interests, which tend to dominate. Consensual long-term solutions are needed, with sufficient common public agreement that they can transcend changes of Government and provide a lasting solution that satisfies all involved and affected, not just serve the interests of airline companies.

The harmful consequences of airport operations are sufficiently important that they cannot be sidelined as technical considerations; they need to be of primary value in the forefront of planning and vision. Once they are fully taken into account, it becomes apparent that the continuing industry and Government focus on growth per se makes no sense in the current environment especially in the system as it exists.

This report outlines the shortcomings of the current decision-making process and previous processes to point towards solutions that will work for everyone from a higher perspective.

2.6 Crash risk

It is quite extraordinary that, yet again, the Government and the industry are trying to push for the further development of the Heathrow airport "hub", for more aircraft and larger aircraft flying over London, without apparently any consideration whatsoever of the consequent increase in the risks of a disastrous crash over London. This risk is already alarmingly high, yet it is never properly or transparently discussed or addressed. Government and industry policy seems to be: ignore it, and hope it will simply go away.

It is totally unacceptable that the current Airports Commission is proposing another unnecessary major development of Heathrow without any prior examination of the consequent and foreseeable increase in crash risk on London.

2.7 Heathrow 24/7?

Furthermore, the Times reports (20 May 2014) that the head of Qatar Airways, a Heathrow Board member and representative of Qatar's sovereign wealth fund, which owns 20% of Heathrow, has proposed that Heathrow should operate all night, 24/7, and quoted him as saying: "If you live under a flight path, I assure you, over a period of time you will not even hear the aircraft passing over your house".

This illustrates that Heathrow Airport patently has no interest in educating its Board members in the experience of the current problems created by its operations. The Board clearly has no idea of the consequences of its operations on the lives of those affected.

London's Mayor, on the other hand, does have more experience, and is quoted as saying: "Heathrow is already the most noise-polluting airport in Europe and it would be catastrophic for the quality of life of Londoners if aircraft were allowed to take-off and land 24 hours a day ... Do these people not deserve a decent night's sleep?"

What the Mayor does not point out is that, even now, with current operations, "these people" do not get "a decent night's sleep". There are, in practice, already virtually no aircraft-free hours.

Time after time, over decades, decision-makers in industry and government have continued to ignore the evidence, that they have presented to them, that the current system is totally dysfunctional and potentially catastrophic. This can continue no longer.

Chapter 3
About the Author

So who is the author of this report?

In a wider context, Gordan describes himself as an expert in seeing the potential for the transformation of systems across different fields of business and politics.

In the context of the current Airports Commission, his first experience was living in Kew with his family for nine years, from 1986 to 1995, under the extension of the two major approach paths to Heathrow.

Over that time, with more aircraft, and larger aircraft, needing longer approach paths, there was a change in the pattern of the approach flight path to Heathrow that focused increasingly more aircraft traffic directly over his house.

In particular, in 1993, two further step changes occurred:

Firstly, there was a change in restrictions regarding night flights, which permitted more air traffic during the night, to the extent that the only hours available for sleep were generally between 12:30 am and 4:30 am – and even this period was interrupted by aircraft: there was no predictable quiet time. There was therefore no relief from this pattern of intense sleep disruption, even on Christmas day.

3.1 The Terminal 5 Inquiry

Secondly, the other thing that happened at that time was that the development of Terminal 5 was proposed in public. Gordan became motivated to be involved with the Terminal 5 Planning Inquiry. Before the inquiry began, he wrote a report on the problems of Heathrow and why (and how) its current operation needed to be improved. This became his passport to entry of the public inquiry as a major participant.

At the start it was expected that the public inquiry was going to last six months. In fact it lasted over three and a half years and became the longest running public planning inquiry ever in the UK.

Acting in a personal capacity and opposing the development on almost all grounds, along with other objecting organisations, Gordan provided around 2,000 pages of evidence to the inquiry. In the process he wrote a series of Heathrow reports based upon the inquiry evidence, which included detailed counter-analysis of most of the topics of the inquiry.

He was particularly surprised to find that he was the only person, and the only body – there were no public organisations doing this – opposing the development of Heathrow on public safety grounds: his was the only voice presenting the issue of the societal risk of an air crash on London.

3.2 Challenging legislation

In 1994 Gordan began a legal case to the European Commission on Human Rights against the UK Government, to challenge the UK legislation that prevents people harmed by noise from aircraft operations from seeking remedy in the UK courts. His case was the foundation for a further case, the 'Hatton' case, and the two consecutive cases took about ten years to come to conclusion between 1994 and 2003.

The end result of these cases was that the UK Government lost the Hatton case in the European Court of Human Rights, but appealed to the Grand Chamber and, with the personal involvement of the UK Attorney General, won the case at this level. It was notable that the Attorney General travelled to Strasbourg and met with the judges before the hearing. It was also notable that the Attorney General's case relied upon evidence which Gordan knew to be untrue. This was the same Attorney General who changed his opinion for Tony Blair on the legality of the invasion of Iraq.

Over time, Gordan also gave evidence to a number of aviation enquiries of the House of Commons Transport Select Committee and gave evidence to aviation enquiries of the European Commission. He also produced and delivered a report entitled "Tomorrow's Civil Aviation – Presenting Solutions to the Problems of UK Air Transport Policy" to the Chair of the Commons Transport Committee and became a Board member of the Aviation Environment Federation. In 1998, he established the Transport Safety Organisation, in the wake of the Ladbroke Grove rail disaster.

For over 35 years, Gordan has been a member of the Royal Institution of Chartered Surveyors and a member of the Royal Society for Public Health. Gordan Glass is the pen name of Gordon Glass.

Gordan's most recent publication is "The President's Legacy", which shows the way to improve processes for global decision-making. Many of the concepts and strategies for solution-finding and decision-making outlined in that book also apply here.

Chapter 4
A Short History of Heathrow and UK Civil Aviation Policy

Heathrow is clearly central to the short-listed proposals of the Airports Commission and it is worth making quick review of how that airport developed. History is not an area of personal interest to the author: the future is much more important than the past. A general overview is useful here, however, even though much more is available from other sources.

Heathrow's origins date back to the 1930s and it was used as an RAF wartime airport. In the early days of the civil airport, after World War II, it was possible to walk from terminal tents to the aircraft. Heathrow was later expanded with the building of Terminals 1, 2 and 3 between its two main runways as air traffic increased, especially with the development of jet and charter travel during the 1960s.

4.1 Terminal 4 – a flawed design

That location of the main terminals between two runways has always been an inherent limitation of Heathrow, requiring road access from the perimeter road and the M4 to be through a tunnel under one of the runways.

At the time of the proposal for Terminal 4, around 1979, there was a public planning inquiry, the "Glidewell Inquiry". Because of the already strong public concern about the adverse consequences of the operations of Heathrow, the result of that inquiry was that Terminal 4 was approved on the basis that it would be "the last major expansion at the airport". Even at that time, the Inspector, Mr Justice Glidewell, said, "It is my view that the present levels of noise around Heathrow are unacceptable in a civilised society". Since then, the noise has spread further out over Greater London.

Terminal 4 was built outside the southern runway and has another inherent limitation: it is necessary to taxi aircraft across one of the main runways from the northern runway in order to get to the Terminal. This meant that use of Terminal 4 interfered with existing runway operations.

4.2 Privatisation

In 1987, the British Airports Authority was privatised and turned into BAA plc; and what was formerly BOAC, as a publicly-owned entity, was also privatised to become British Airways plc.

4.3 Terminal 5

The next major development was the proposal of Terminal 5. This development was proposed on the basis that, in order to deal with the lack of airspace and runway capacity, there was a need for much larger aircraft. The development of Terminal 5 allowed Heathrow to be reconfigured on this basis.

At the Terminal 5 inquiry, BAA plc made a clear statement that they saw no need for a third runway, even though at the time it was demonstrated that British Airways owned most of the land to the north of the airport where a third runway was already planned. British Airways had previously bought this land cheaply from London Borough of Hillingdon on the basis that it was going to be made into a public park – but this park never materialised.

At the conclusion of the Terminal 5 public inquiry the Inspector confirmed the evidence of the various objections that the adverse consequences of the airport would grow with the development, but he decided to approve the development anyway.

4.4 A third runway?

After the development of Terminal 5 there were various proposals for a third runway at Heathrow and, after a flawed consultation process, the concept of a third runway was approved by Labour Government in 2009.

In the run-up to the 2010 elections, because of the strength of public opposition, the Conservative Party pledged to overturn this decision and not support the proposal for a third runway. However, once in power, the same Government changed this pledge to “not in this parliament” and then appointed the current Airports Commission.

This Commission has produced an Interim Report, which focuses mainly on development of Heathrow. The report sidelines the idea of an Estuary airport, as proposed by the Mayor of London and others, although the interim report left open the possibility for review of that decision in the Commission’s final report.

4.5 Government policy and decisions

In terms of Government policy there has been very little effective and proper management of aviation policy. There have been only two White Papers on UK airports policy (1985 and 2003) and the policy has been designed to enable the development of civil aviation in a relatively uncontrolled manner.

This has been further exacerbated by Government's Aviation Policy Framework of March 2013, which still focuses on "supporting growth" and "securing the benefits of aviation" and the now-out-dated concept of "balance" to "mitigate" negative impacts. The Government's paper notes, for example, as a key fact: "*London … delivers the connections UK PLC (sic) requires*". Quite what "UK Plc" is or what "it" requires is unspecified. Similarly, the Framework claims "*Our major airports face a medium- and longer-term capacity and connectivity challenge which the Government must tackle*". No they don't, actually. From where did the Government get this thinking, along with the assumption that Government must tackle it?

The Government seems to be working on the basis that it is still running the old nationalised industry from the 1970s so that BAA Plc is still the old British Airports Authority and needs to be protected from the public. In fact, one of the major purposes of government has always been to protect the public from being harmed by large, profit-chasing corporations.

The conceptual thinking of our Government has not improved for over 40 years: the phraseology is much the same. Societal risks still do not appear to be considered a factor worthy of discussion in the "Aviation Policy Framework". The development of civil aviation has been left up to the airport operators and the airlines to do largely what they want, regardless of the consequences.

There has been no specific regulating body responsible for dealing with the adverse consequences of airport operations or to decide on overall policy. As a result, the airport and airline operators have mainly driven the direction of development, whilst the objections of the public affected by their operations have been effectively over-ridden in decision-making processes.

After the Terminal 5 public inquiry lasted over three and a half years – mainly because of the strength of opposition to the proposals – the UK Government subsequently decided that decisions on future major infrastructure development projects should be made prior to any planning inquiry process. This change was made in order to reduce the potential for public objection and public influence in the decision-making process and to speed up that decision-making process.

Hence the current Airports Commission was set up by the current Government, with a mandate from the Government to pursue the Government's stated objective of "growth" of the industry "hub" without proper public debate or analysis of the adverse consequences.

In particular, it appears that the Government still wants the subject of crash risk to be ignored in favour of "growth" of the UK's "hub": that the risks of aircraft crashes on London should not be mentioned in its policy document and that they should not be discussed before deciding on more development at Heathrow. This seems to be a similar strategy to the wars in Afghanistan and Iraq: bury the bodies and muddle along.

There has been remarkable lack of consistency in the structure of decision-making processes related to the UK Air Transport System in general and to Heathrow in particular. No body appears to be in charge. No vision or purpose. No clear values. Time for change.

4.6 Conclusion

The conclusion from the history of Heathrow is that each major step in its development has compounded the inherent flaws, problems and adverse consequences which have all arisen from the fact that Heathrow is in the wrong location for a major hub airport.

Furthermore, the focus of decision-making relating to Heathrow airport has been driven by the main airlines at Heathrow in order to deepen their monopoly of the hub – seemingly regardless of the adverse consequences, both to the people of London and the rest of the country.

The legal position supports this approach; not only with a Government policy in favour of the growth of the industry without regard to the purpose of this growth or the values underlying it; but also with the legal power to challenge this policy on the basis of the adverse consequences removed from the people who are harmed by these consequences.

There has been no system or body to look consistently at sensible alternatives to those driven by the convenience of the industry. For decades, the Government has actively focused on the needs of the airlines and against the needs of the people affected.

The current Airports Commission is continuing this highly unsatisfactory and flawed process by proposing yet more development of Heathrow which is not only unnecessary, but which will further exacerbate the associated risks and harm. In fact the short-listed proposals at Heathrow seem so ridiculously unworkable and ill-thought-through that they seem to be "decoy" proposals for some other plan to appear later for Heathrow.

In its process the Commission has, for no justifiable reasons, sidelined the estuary airport proposals, which are the only development proposals that could entirely remove the risks and harm to people on the ground.

It is time this process was transformed: to serve instead the needs of the people at risk. The industry can afford to have the necessary changes imposed upon it. Will the Airports Commission rise to the challenge of backing the recommendations in this report?

Chapter 5
The Need for Transformation

The concept of transformation is based on the understanding that continuous growth is, in principle, unsustainable. This is well known in system architecture, where systems are designed to work over the long term, and it is observable in nature and in economic cycles. Typically there is a period of linear growth and then the system changes as growth becomes exponential and unsustainable; once a certain size is reached the system needs operate in a different way.

What is needed for transformation in this situation is a *step change* – a completely different way of doing things. This involves a *change of state* to a different way of operating. If a step change does not happen when growth gets to a point where it becomes unsustainable, then typically what occurs is that the system becomes self-destructive or system failure occurs. In particular, hubs – critical points around which a system revolves – tend to break down from congestion and overload. Usually this doesn't happen at first with failure of the whole system: it shows up initially with a seemingly small failure in part of the system. Once the growth reaches a critical point, this then leads to failure of the whole by progressive collapse of the system.

Transformation, as a step change in human systems, is generally enabled through deeper understanding via insight. There is an 'aha' moment where a new, different and better understanding occurs, which involves changing away from "this is the way we've always done things". Insight results in a step change of understanding and belief.

5.1 Historical examples of transformation

There are various examples in history in which such step changes can be seen, particularly in science.

Arguably one of the most important is the Copernican Revolution, which started in the 1500s, when Copernicus realised that the sun didn't go around the Earth, but that the Earth went around the sun.

As in this example, such a belief change is often initially seen as heretical, or ridiculous. It counters existing beliefs and assumptions and understanding. Copernicus' insight could not be accepted by the religious powers of the time and, indeed, took a long time to be accepted by society as a whole.

5.2 New beliefs take hold

Then usually what happens with such a change of belief is that it gradually becomes common understanding: that there is a new truth out there that was not previously recognised and the current way of doing things needs to change in light of it. It is hard now to imagine that anyone would believe in the concept of a flat Earth, with the oceans running off the edge, yet this was what many people believed in the past. Now that we fly around the Earth, it is obvious. We can see that it's not flat.

At the point of insight a reversal happens. There is a change of perspective and in that moment, everything seems to change and yet nothing changes. A new understanding and a new thinking is set in train and new and different outcomes occur.

In most cases, this insight is driven by conflict that is generated from feedback from a system that is no longer functioning well and from the growth of the problems that occur as a result.

5.3 Breakdown of democratic system

An example is the system of human governance, and how this operates here. In a fully functioning democracy, the concept of feedback is built in, where the views from the people at the bottom of the hierarchy should be fed back to the people at the top of the hierarchy to result in change in decisions.

But this system tends not to work effectively in the UK, and particularly not in the transport sector, because Government policy is not geared towards the needs of the people. Current policies favour the development of business and there is no democratically responsible body in charge of the decision-making process. The Airports Commission is a deliberate system to side-step the democratic process.

The political system has been distorted by business involvement; politicians are lobbied by businesses, given gifts and free air travel. Placement on decision-making committees is in the power of the few. A further factor is that a formal bar exists in the Civil Aviation Act against legal action and remedy from harm, so that members of the public have little or no ability to have their voice heard.

5.4 Moving to higher values

It is clear to see that the next step change in the UK air transport sector has been prevented from happening and is still being prevented from happening because the democratic process is not working effectively. It has long been obvious – at least since the proposals for the development of the Maplin Airport in the 1970s, and reiterated in the public inquiries for Terminal 4 in the 1980s and Terminal 5 in the 1990s – that Heathrow is in the wrong location for an airport with very high volumes of traffic, and should not continue to be developed. For similar reasons, the French decided to build Charles de Gaulle airport in the 1970s, with its location outside Paris. A new vision of a more sensible future is needed, but the UK has tended to suffer from Governments that have not embraced the concept of vision and have not been smart enough to see the truth and act upon it.

The truth is that there are simpler and better solutions for an ideal outcome but, because the Government has long been blinkered and driven by the undue influence of the industry, the step change and transformation of the system that has been needed has not been able to happen. The Heathrow-based system has already reached beyond its maximum effectiveness. Something fundamental needs to change in Government thinking.

The same blinkered thinking continues in the UK Government decision-making processes. The world has moved on to higher values, but the UK Government has not. It still drives decision-making on outdated assumptions, such as on the basis that it tries to further the interest of certain companies, rather than protect the health and safety of the people.

This urgently needs to change: Britain has many creative people who are at the forefront of understanding and skill in transformational change. These people tend not to be found in process- and procedure-driven organisations, such as government and industry, where the mantra tends to be “this is the way we’ve always done it”, but such people exist, ready to contribute, if the system will let them.

Chapter 6
A different approach is needed

6.1 Remove the focus on one hub

One obvious transformative solution now is the same as it was in the 1970s: to develop another purpose-built hub in a more appropriate location. Another hub could be anywhere, it could be in the Thames Estuary, it could be in Scotland for example, or it could be at another offshore location around the UK.

Yet, also, another hub is not essential. A more Euro-centric solution could be to move more focus to the other European airport hubs, which have greater room for expansion. As the Commission's Interim Report points out, there are already direct links from the UK regional airports to other European hubs. So this last move is already happening. It would be sensible to encourage that move to grow without developing any UK hub.

There is a strong body of opinion in favour of an overall reduction in the UK reliance on air transport and on an increase in the cost of flying over other forms of transport, to reduce the passenger throughput at all the airports around the UK.

Whilst it is not necessary to build another hub, doing so could, importantly, permit a progressive reduction in air traffic, and consequent risks, at Heathrow.

6.2 Reduce air traffic at Heathrow

The possible reduction of air traffic at Heathrow is an important concept to consider. The Airports Commission Report seems to have only considered either the development of Heathrow or the closure of Heathrow; it has not considered the obvious prospect of making Heathrow an effective local and business airport.

The industry acknowledges that it wants to focus on the business traffic at Heathrow. Then let it do so. If, as the industry argues, business people do not want to move to another hub or fly through another hub, but want to use Heathrow, then let them continue to do so. In that case, business-only flights to long-haul destinations would develop, with some economy seats for London-local passengers. This is a perfectly feasible prospect as Heathrow has operated at far lower levels of air traffic in the past. Air traffic could easily be halved at Heathrow to the levels that existed prior to the Glidewell Inquiry in 1980, below 275,000 movements per annum.

A level of reduction of this magnitude and more would be necessary to reduce the levels of risk and harm to more acceptable levels, although it must be acknowledged that the entire closure of Heathrow would be a more effective and preferable solution in the long term.

6.3 Remove transfer passengers

A key factor in reducing the traffic at Heathrow is to remove the industry focus on transfer passengers. Traditionally, transfer passengers have formed a large percentage of the passenger traffic through Heathrow – some 40-50% of passengers. But transfer passengers do not want to be there, they want to be somewhere else, by definition. It makes no sense to have people passing through an overloaded airport when they could be travelling directly, or via a less busy hub.

It would also be possible to remove the non-local passengers. At the moment the monopoly of Heathrow means that many passengers need to travel over long distances in order to fly long-haul from Heathrow. That should not need to happen. They could fly from local airports if the monopoly of Heathrow were reduced, or they could use another hub.

If taxation costs of air travel were raised, higher-spending business passengers would be more likely to pay it than other passengers. In other words, it is possible to raise the cost of air travel through taxation to remove transfer passenger traffic and so to halve the passenger throughput at Heathrow, virtually at a stroke.

6.4 Provide an alternative hub

The Thames Estuary has long been considered the preferred location for a new hub airport. There are off-shore airports around the world, and they have been built specifically to reduce the risks to health and safety of local residents. Various proposed airport projects have been raised for the Thames Estuary but without any enabling Government decision to proceed. If Government, for example, just made a clear decision that it wanted to see an airport in the Thames Estuary, rather than the development of Heathrow, then the industry, the operators and the architects would get together to come up with the right solution themselves.

The Government has missed many opportunities throughout the last forty years of airport development. The current proposal by Foster and Partners, for a new airport on the Isle of Grain, for example – inexplicably dismissed by the Airports Commission – would have huge additional benefits for the London region: the incorporation of a new Thames Barrier, wave and tidal power generation and better transport connections with road and rail to existing infrastructure. This proposal would have major advantages for the South-East.

6.5 No arguments against the Estuary

The Commission's stated reasons for dismissing the prospect of an Estuary airport do not stand up to analysis. They are (reference paragraph 43 of its Interim Report):

- Expense
- Environmental issues
- Requirement for extensive surface access infrastructure

These can be reduced to two main objections:

- Funding: there is no reason investment could not be found to build the airport and the important associated societal infrastructure;

- The prospect of the displacement of birds. The simple choice is do we continue to harm the lives of people or do we displace birds? The idea that the disturbance of birds is far more important than harm to people is a very strange policy concept.

In its Interim Report, the Commission says that the wildlife policy in the Thames could be changed on grounds of public safety; and public safety, after all, is the greatest reason for putting a new airport hub in the Estuary.

6.6 The unique benefits of the Estuary

It would be relatively easy to build a new airport in the shallow water within the Thames Estuary; but the main argument that makes the Thames Estuary an obvious solution is that there would be no harmful consequences, to human beings on the ground, from noise or accident risk.

Only an offshore location provides this unique benefit, and this is the reason why off-shore locations have been chosen in other countries. Is there some hidden agenda why the Airports Commission wants to bury this obvious and beneficial solution?

6.7 The risks of a crash on London

At the moment, the risks of a crash on London are unacceptably high – at one crash about every 10 years - with all of the disastrous consequences that would entail. The more aircraft flying over London, and the larger the aircraft, and the closer together they become, the higher the risks. Over the ocean, the consequences at least would be greatly reduced, totally removing the risk, which already exists in London, to people on the ground.

Heathrow is already seriously harming the people who live in the greater London area. Previous inquiries have made this abundantly clear, and local parliamentarians are well aware of their constituents' views on the matter. These consequences will only increase with further expansion. Reduction in traffic at Heathrow, combined with the use of another hub in a well-chosen location, will have benefits for all.

If it is considered necessary to build another hub it makes sense to do so in a location that removes the harmful consequences.

6.8 The closure of Heathrow

The Airports Commission says (paragraph 44): "An estuary airport would require closure of Heathrow for commercial reasons".

The Airports Commission appears to have jumped to this conclusion without considering that Heathrow could continue to function commercially as a specialised local business airport with greatly reduced air traffic throughput.

However, the most compelling justification for the reduction and complete closure of Heathrow is to remove the current – and growing – risks to the health and safety of Greater Londoners.

The Government's operating agreement with Heathrow Airport Ltd already enables it to close down the airport.

Chapter 7
No Third Runway

7.1 Why 'No' to a third runway?

The quick answer is that a third runway at Heathrow is not actually necessary, even though airlines may argue that it is. Indeed, at the Terminal 5 inquiry, BAA plc argued that it would not be necessary.

The main purpose of a third runway, especially as it is likely to be a shorter runway, would be to increase the use of Heathrow as a transfer hub feeder facility. This would mean that short-haul aircraft could arrive from other UK and European airports and transfer more passengers to long-haul flights in more, larger, aircraft using the two existing main runways.

A third runway would therefore merely increase the number of transfer passengers flying through Heathrow, when what is required at Heathrow is a reduction in the number of transfer passengers.

The effect of a third runway would be to introduce new approach and takeoff flight paths for the new runway, make air traffic more complex, and therefore more liable to error; it would increase noise, disturbance and public risk from aircraft flying over London.

It would be far better if this transfer and resultant increase in transfer passengers happened elsewhere, at a new or alternative hub. Then, rather than developing Heathrow, it would be possible to reduce the throughput of Heathrow.

The result would be a reduction in the number of large aircraft, a reduction in the affected areas of London, a reduction in air congestion, a reduction in the need for multimode operation (the simultaneous use of both runways for departing and arriving aircraft) and a consequent reduction in the risks of disaster on London.

7.2 Bonus opportunity

Once a decision is made not to build a third runway, it creates a golden opportunity to build a large area of social housing in the green belt in place of the proposed third runway location, north of existing Heathrow. This land will have good access to Heathrow, the M4 and to Hayes & Harlington Crossrail Rail Station.

7.3 Foreign ownership

The Government has long been intent on the expansion of Heathrow. But BAA Plc is now not a British owned business. So why is the Government intent on helping it to expand? Why should the Government help a foreign corporation expand and increase the consequent harm to residents?

7.4 In summary

The benefits of increasing controls and limits on the operations of Heathrow are that it would be better for business passengers and London-local passengers, it would be better for the residents of London, it would reduce the monopoly of Heathrow by certain airlines and the effect on other regional airports – indeed, it would enable the development of other regional airports and so would be better for current non-London passengers as well.

An Estuary hub would mean having one airport west of London and one airport east of London; there would be far better rail access connections to the Continent from a hub in the Estuary; and there would be the commensurate side benefits of additional infrastructure development for the UK, associated with an Estuary airport.

Chapter 8
Problems with the Focus on Heathrow

It is not hard to see why the airlines, and British Airways in particular, want to keep developing Heathrow: to increase their monopoly grip and profit. This is standard industry practice for a mature business. However, should this desire for corporate profitability be supported by Government policy, in the face of the following problems? The following is a basic list of some of the problems with the current use of the air transport system, especially based, as it is, on the outdated notion of a Heathrow hub.

Problem #1 - The wrong location

As shown in the history section, Heathrow has evolved over time since World War II in relatively uncontrolled fashion; and in the process a lot of harm has been created for the residents affected by it.

At the beginning it was a small local airport. Planes approached from very close to the airport and landed there without affecting many people. But over time and with larger aircraft, the extent of the air traffic movements, and particularly the longer approach path, have affected more and more people – in terms of noise and, more importantly, in terms of the risk and danger of a disastrous crash on London.

This should be compared with Paris, for example, where there is a law that over-flight of Paris is not permitted – which was why Charles de Gaulle Airport was built in its current strategic location in the 1970s, at the same time as the UK Government proposed Maplin and then decided against it.

Problem #2 - The wrong design

The way Heathrow was originally designed, it was constrained, as mentioned in the history, because access to the terminals needed to be via a tunnel under one of the runways. Inherent limitations were built into the design of Heathrow which have made it far from efficient in operation, especially with only two runways.

The same happened with both Terminal 4 and Terminal 5. Although with Terminal 5 access was created from the M25, the terminal was put at the end of the runways, between the two runways. This is one of the most dangerous places to have a terminal in terms of risk from crashes.

The idea of building a third runway to create another runway north of the airport or even to extend the existing runway would create another approach and take-off path and interfere with the air traffic controls for the other two runways. There are proposals for complicated Air Traffic Control techniques to deal with an extra runway but the public safety case has not been raised in considering these proposals. The fact that a third runway would greatly add both more noise and more risk is without question.

Problem #3 - The wrong industry policy

Industry policy has been to maximise the growth of passenger numbers, mainly because the industry sees increasing the number of passengers as increasing its income and profitability. This has been driven by airlines, in particular. Even twenty years ago there were sixty-four flights a day to Paris, many departing at the same time with different airlines. Many flights from Heathrow are not fully occupied as a result. Many passengers are in fact flying for free (or virtually for free, with air-miles) on part-occupied planes.

The focus has been to squeeze more and more passengers into more and more aircraft – usually in cramped and unhealthy seating positions – at ever lower-prices, and to try and attract them from further and further around; but more passengers mean larger aircraft and more noise and more resultant risk.

Problem #4 - Wrong Government policy

The UK Government policy has also historically been to focus on increasing air traffic. This seems to have been driven by the mandate of the Department for Transport to do so, for reasons of its own. This mandate is clearly outdated; it is now recognised for all transport modalities that growth is not the answer.

Indeed, after years redesigning country roads to enable cars to travel more quickly, in many areas speed limits have been introduced on the roads to reduce the speed of traffic and other controls have been introduced in road transport policy to reduce the number of cars on the road – or rather, to reduce the increase in the number of cars. The same reasoning is now valid for air transport.

The approach of the Government and Airports Commission relies on forecasting passenger demand, but overlooks the basic economic theory that demand is dependent on price. Many airlines now give virtually free flights to many passengers and if they continue to do so, demand will naturally increase. In common with other maturing industries, such as communication, the price of air travel has been falling to the level that it is now often effectively zero, apart from taxes and fees. Is forecast demand in future therefore to be based on all passengers flying free?

Problem #5 – Wrong reasoning

The industry uses many arguments that distort Government policy, because the industry only provides one side of the argument and ignores the greater downside. For example:

- the idea that air travel brings in tourists which improves the balance of payment. In fact the other side is missed out, which is that British airlines take out more British passengers than they bring in foreign passengers.

- the idea that investment is brought into the country, whereas in fact the focus of airlines is to provide businesses with flights to emerging markets; businesses invest their money in those emerging markets, so there is more outward investment from British passengers than there is inward investment on British airlines.

- it is often argued by the industry that jobs will increase as airports are developed, but the evidence shows that over time more automation is brought in, for example in baggage handling etc, and that there is a continuing reduction in jobs. This can be seen very clearly over time with Heathrow.

Problem #6 – The wrong focus

Most importantly, there is no focus by the Government on alleviating harm. There is no separate body responsible for the reduction of public risk and harm commensurate with the Government policy for growth and expansion – and there ought to be, particularly as public remedy has been removed in law. Indeed, there needs to be a body specifically charged to deal with, and remedy, public harm from air transport.

Quite apart from Heathrow, aviation is a very noisy activity. There needs to be, and could easily be, far more stringent noise constraints to reduce the harm from all types of aircraft.

Problem #7 – The wrong regulation

The principle focus for regulation by the Civil Aviation Authority is economic regulation. This works in favour of the airlines by keeping landing charges low, thereby aiming to increase passenger numbers and growth. In doing so it also increases the risk and the harm from extra passenger throughput.

Apart from some controls on total aircraft numbers and night noise, little attention is paid to the harm being created, with no regular review or monitoring of it.

The CAA made clear at the Terminal 5 inquiry that it was not responsible for public safety and societal risk. Its mandate is for passenger safety only. There are no public bodies responsible for the proper regulation of aircraft noise or for societal risk from aircraft.

Such controls as exist relating to aircraft noise nevertheless permit copious exceptions to the rules. Any Government controls are simply moved by Government when they become inconvenient to the industry.

Problem #8 – Flaws in noise mapping

Noise mapping is produced for the area around Heathrow but the noise measurement process is flawed; the system greatly reduces the effect of the numbers of aircraft – on a logarithmic basis – even though it is the increased numbers of aircraft that causes the increased harm from noise, such as sleep disturbance, stopping conversations, affecting the effectiveness of children's learning, and the health impacts on the mind that are still being researched.

Another flaw in the noise mapping system is that it is constructed from a theoretical model, not from actual measurements on the ground. This model does not allow for, for example, the increased noise that is generated by aging aircraft.

Problem #9 – The wrong system for noise measurement

The noise measurement techniques used also deliberately cut out low frequency noise, below 50 Hz; low frequency noise is known to affect the internal organs and to be a significant factor in shaking existing structures and buildings, potentially compromising their integrity. It is at low frequency that most of the noise power is transmitted, yet this is deliberately cut out from the measurement process. The conclusion is that the actual levels of noise are being deliberately downplayed by this noise measurement policy, which makes the mapping meaningless.

An example of this is that the halting of the Concorde flights – only one or two a day – enabled a disproportionate increase in the numbers of aircraft without appearing to increase the noise levels over Heathrow and the surrounding area, as indicated by the mapping.

So what does it mean to live under the flight path in terms of noise? Half of the daily air traffic through Heathrow travels down one of two flight paths, with alternation between these paths. This means that half of the air traffic going through Heathrow travels over small numbers of people, approximately one every minute or less for half of the day, between 4-5 a.m. and midnight. For many people, at its peak, the noise is at a level to impact on conversation, typically halting a conversation until the aircraft has passed overhead. The duration of the noise is such that when one aircraft has past the next one can be heard arriving.

Some people appear to become accustomed to this level of noise. For many others it causes ongoing stress. The health consequences can have a serious impact on people's lives, but it is beyond the scope of this report to document them.

Problem #10 – The wrong measures of harm

The dictionary defines “harm” as physical or mental injury. The law is clear in its endeavours to prevent harm to people. However, it is no body’s responsibility to measure harm, track harm or remedy harm in wider society caused by aircraft operations.

Decades ago, the UK Government carried out limited research into the consequences of aircraft noise, but measured only levels of disturbance and annoyance, and did so in a very superficial manner. It measured neither physical nor mental injury from aircraft noise.

Yet this outdated and discredited research continues to be the foundation for both Government and industry theoretical assessment of harm from aircraft activities.

There is an abundance of research and empirical experience to show that noise can have extremely harmful consequences on the human body, especially at high volume levels and also at very low frequency levels (which are deliberately excluded from the aircraft noise measurement regime).

There is a growing body of evidence that aircraft noise can seriously interfere with mental processing in the human brain – especially in ability to learn and be mentally productive.

The military is aware that low frequency noise generators can be effective weapons against human bodies and can be very harmful to internal organs.

There has been copious research to demonstrate the extreme consequences of sleep deprivation and interruption, especially under continuous exposure over long periods.

Such conditions are considered to be torture conditions. Yet these are the conditions that very many people are exposed to constantly in Greater London. Yet also, this is the very harm for which the Government continues to maintain a statutory bar against examination in the UK Courts.

It is not surprising that MPs continue to receive many complaints about aircraft operations: the author of this report has himself suffered the extreme consequences. Indeed the consequences can be, and are in certain circumstances, extremely debilitating and seriously affect everyday life on a continuous basis.

Yet no body is responsible for investigating or responding to this harm or for providing any remedial process. The matter continues to be institutionally ignored. It is time that this quite outrageously inhuman Government approach to its citizens is permanently outlawed. It is time that a new public body is established with a mandate to remedy the often-serious harm – that is physical and mental injury – caused by aircraft operations.

Problem #11 – The wrong controls for health and safety

Health and safety is a key policy consideration in Government and the Health and Safety Executive is very stringent at setting standards and making sure that industry complies with them. But this only applies to businesses and their employees. The Heath and Safety Executive do not have any control over the risks of aircraft operations on the local population.

This effectively means that there is no body looking after the health and safety consequences for the people who live around Heathrow or who live in London who might be affected by the societal crash risks and consequences. The health risks and consequences are those associated with noise, already referred to, and also pollution.

The Airports Commission took into consideration climate change possibilities and so has presumably considered some aspects of pollution; but there are secondary aspects relating to pollution: things like fuel residue that is deposited in the area.

It should be remembered that solid objects are sometimes dropped off aircraft, varying from blocks of frozen urine, to locking keys falling out of wheel bays – and even stowaways falling out of wheel bays – when undercarriages are lowered on approach.

These consequences are known to Government and to the CAA but they are usually quickly covered up if possible. For example, when properties are damaged, compensation is paid on the basis that there is no publicity about the incidents.

Problem #12 – The risk of crashes

A very great concern is the public risk of the consequences of an air crash which arise from living under a flight path along which half of the aircraft approaching Heathrow pass. The risk of an air accident may be one in a million, if one is a passenger in an aircraft, but, for a person living under a million flights, that risk becomes much more material.

The public risk of living under a flight path is a difficult topic to discuss in public, because most of the people who are at risk can only live in denial of that risk; therefore they do not want to talk about it – they have to pretend that there is no risk. In the Terminal 5 public inquiry the author demonstrated that, according to crash statistics, the risk of an aircraft crash over London is within the region of one every ten years.

It could be argued that therefore there should have been two crashes in the last twenty years, but the fact that there haven't been does not invalidate the statistical analysis.

Who is responsible for measuring these risks and controlling these risks? Who is responsible for paying for the research? Where is the public discussion about these risks?

At the moment there doesn't appear to be any independent body responsible for managing these risks and indeed it is a notable omission from the Airports Commission Interim Report in December 2013 that **there is no serious mention of safety – let alone public safety** – or of the risks of a crash on London. It is inconceivable that a Commission such as this should propose to increase the operation of Heathrow with all the attendant increased complexity without a proper prior analysis of the public risks and safety cases involved.

The Airports Commission Interim Report rightly proposes that there should be an aviation noise authority; in the same way it needs to propose an independent, publicly-funded aviation public risk authority or public health and safety authority.

Problem #13 – A lack of planning controls

The majority of expansion at UK airports is carried out under the Planning General Development Order and does not need specific Planning Consent. It is only when there are certain specific proposals, such as the development of a new terminal or a new runway, that the operations of the airports are examined in the public eye.

There is no continuous control or monitoring over the expansion of airports, in the same way that there is no continuous control over the management of the public health and safety risks. Indeed, the approval of Terminal 5 and the reconfiguration of Heathrow has enabled another round of continuous growth in passenger numbers and larger aircraft. This latest round of increases in passenger throughput has only just started and itself will increase risks, even without further development.

Problem #14 – Lack of funds for opposing proposed developments

When it comes to matters like planning inquiries – and the current Airports Commission – there is a serious imbalance in the ability to provide detailed evidence, between the industry and the Government, on the one hand, and the local authorities and the members of the public, on the other hand.

In the Terminal 5 inquiry, for example, there was a long string of industry witnesses paid for by the industry; they were paid for their time to be there, with polished documents and evidence written on their behalf and provided for them to read as witnesses. The same was true for Government witnesses and for the CAA, as far as they were involved.

When it came to local authorities, those local authorities had to pay their own costs. As the inquiry continued, they were unable to continue to spend the money required to provide the evidence and the legal representation that was necessary; they ran out of money and could not continue to pay their one joint barrister. That meant they could not continue to oppose the development within certain sectors of the inquiry.

Similarly, the few public representative organisations, like the Anti-Noise Association, who were opposing the development, had virtually no resources to pay for research to counter the industry evidence.

When it came to the public safety topic, as the inquiry had been running for years, the local authorities did not have the funding to pay for presenting their evidence. So the author, as an unpaid individual, realised that he was the only person who was left to address the crash risk to London. The local planning authority's barrister said: "Good luck, Mr Glass, we're depending on you".

It seemed extraordinary that it should fall to one individual, indeed, one unpaid individual, to carry out the necessary work and analysis of the evidence and statistics in order to safeguard London from a crash risk.

If there were a proper body to carry out this work and proper funding available to articulate the public interest, there would be more of an equitable inquiry and decision-making process than there is currently. At the moment, all the evidence is one-sided and stacked in favour of the industry. This does not make for balanced decision-making.

Problem #15 - The lack of democratic and legal control

As things currently stand in the UK, members of the public have no legal remedy against aircraft noise or risk. This has been deliberately removed and barred by Government legislation. The author challenged this in the European Court of Human Rights – with others – but the legislation remains, despite the fact that that European Court was obviously concerned that this was unreasonable.

It is clear that the feedback of the consequences of harm have now reached governmental level through the political process, but even so, the intense and continuous long-term industry lobbying of politicians and civil servants, and the benefits the industry provides them, clearly influences politicians to support the industry against those who are affected by the operations of airports and air traffic.

The democratic process is diminished also by the prevalent tendency to give preference to an unharmed majority rather than the needs of a harmed minority. The Conservative Party made a clear statement that they would not approve a third runway and yet it did not take the current Prime Minister very long to change his mind about this once in power, to change the phrase to “not in this Parliament” and be persuaded to appoint an Airports Commission to examine the very same proposal.

For a long time, the majority of local authorities and parliamentary representatives around Heathrow have been set against the continuing growth of Heathrow because of public pressure, but this has not had any effect on policy. Why is this? The democratic process is not functioning properly.

Problem #16 – Lack of control over terrorist risk

In general, terrorism is not taken into account in risk assessments or planning decisions. At the Terminal 5 inquiry, the inspector dismissed the subject as irrelevant. However, the risk of another Lockerbie-style incident over London continues as the UK has no control over security failures at foreign airports.

The recent incident of a Malay aircraft (Flight MH370) has highlighted the risks, more especially the possibility of hijack by remote-control as, after 9/11, Boeing was reported to have provided cockpit-override facilities from the ground. This incident has not yet been resolved.

These risks are real and of great concern. There is little that can be done about them in practice by UK bodies, but this is not a reason to ignore them. It need hardly be said that, with virtually all air movements to Heathrow flying over London, these risks are serious.

Problem #17 – Shortage of fuel

One of the most significant concerns with respect to aircraft crash risk over London comes from the prospect of fuel shortages. In January 2008, flight BA38, crash-landed short of the runway at Heathrow. In this case, ice crystals were blamed for apparent fuel starvation, but air accident reports over the years document a number of incidents where aircraft had insufficient fuel to complete their flights.

It is easy to see that BA 38 might not have made it to the airport for its crash-landing: it could have been on London. It is not uncommon for air-traffic controllers to be asked to give priority for aircraft to land at Heathrow on the basis of shortage of fuel.

Fuel is expensive, and airlines are under significant economic pressure to save expenditure on fuel. However, lack of fuel is not factored into aviation crash statistics, only actual crashes. Almost-crashing on London does not count.

Chapter 9
The Heathrow Myths

The aviation industry has been very good over many years at pedalling a number of myths. These are listed here because they need much deeper consideration than they have been given to date. This is not the place for that deeper consideration. Instead, the overview response is assembled for each, as a starting point.

Myth #1 – "Safety is our first priority"

It isn't. As stated previously, there is no body responsible for the management of public safety, especially in relationship to proposed developments such as a third runway at Heathrow. This is evident from the Airports Commission Interim Report, where public safety and societal risk seem to have been almost totally overlooked. Societal risk has been designed to fall into a corporate black hole where nobody can be held responsible – for a crash on London, for example.

Myth #2 – "Aircraft are getting quieter"

The evidence is not that aircraft are getting quieter – there is no such thing as a quiet jumbo jet overhead. In fact, the statistics show that, over the years, aircraft are getting quieter per passenger, but as they are getting larger they are still perceived as noisier per aircraft and noisier overall than previously. More importantly, each aircraft passing overhead still instils fear and anxiety.

Myth #3 – "The noise area is reducing"

The Airports Commission gives great play to this myth, but the truth is, as stated previously, that this is because of the erroneous noise measuring system, which is designed to ensure that the noise area appears to reduce, even though the number of aircraft increases, and the total noise effect from them increases. This is achieved by:

a) not measuring some of the output

b) calculating it in such a way as to diminish it

c) mapping the area on a theoretical basis only

Myth #4 – "Double glazing is the answer"

Heathrow Airport Ltd has recently invested money in double and triple glazing the houses of people affected by aircraft noise. This is telling. Even though the industry claims that the noise theoretically has been reduced, it is only recently that the company has found it necessary to provide double and triple glazing. Something doesn't add up here. The noise measurement and mapping system is actually designed to be totally misleading.

Of course, double and triple glazing are not the answer because they don't stop the interference of aircraft in people's enjoyment of the local area or their gardens. Indeed, they do not even stop all the noise inside the building. Aircraft can still be disturbing, even with additional glazing.

Myth #5 – "Effective controls over night flights"

Again, it has already been stated that the controls over night flights only operate to provide some four to five hours sleep per night; but even this period is interrupted by many permitted exceptions such as mail flights and certain other movements, so these controls are not controls and are meaningless for most people affected by night flights. The resultant stress of sleep interruption can be akin to torture.

Myth #6 – "The aviation industry brings inward investment"

Again, as stated previously, the reality is that almost certainly more investment goes out to emerging markets and other countries than comes into the UK through aviation. The industry only presents one side of the economic argument, not the downside. Nobody outside the industry has sufficient funds to demonstrate the truth that the economic arguments of the industry are flawed.

However, as a brief illustration of the imbalances in the flow of funds through travel, the Office of National Statistics is reported to indicate that British visits abroad total 58.5m whilst overseas visits to the UK total 32.8m, and spending by British visitors abroad is £34.9bn, whilst overseas visitors spend £21bn in the UK. On both measures, air travel provides a net loss to the UK.

Myth #7 – "Business needs Heathrow" or "London needs Heathrow"

Neither of these is true. London may need an airport, and businesses may need an airport, but the exact location does not matter too much, neither does the size. An Estuary airport would serve the needs of London just as well as Heathrow does.

Myth #8 – "Transfer passengers are essential"

No, they are not. Transfer passengers do not want to be at Heathrow, they want to be somewhere else; whilst it is useful for airlines to have more passengers, they add nothing positive, yet they add to the harm that is caused by the consequent doubling of passenger numbers, increased air traffic and increased aircraft size.

Myth #9 – "London needs a hub airport"

No it doesn't. Actually, systems engineering shows that hubs cannot last very long before they break down with congestion and overload. The question is, is the hub model going to be dispensed with before we have serious a breakdown, possibly crashes in London; or will we have to wait until after these have happened for people to wake up to the inevitable? The system has reached beyond safe risk capacity and needs to be transformed.

Myth #10 – "More destinations are essential"

No, they are not. It is perfectly possible to – and indeed many people do – fly to smaller destinations by flying to an intermediate airport local to their destination. This still gives effective connectivity. If more destinations were essential, consider the logical conclusion: is it essential that aircraft should fly to every airport in the world from

Heathrow? Is that the industry's objective? It is obvious that this is neither necessary nor beneficial. Similarly, many UK passengers prefer to fly via European airports other than Heathrow. It is only the airlines that try to pull more passengers through Heathrow.

Myth #11 – "The CAA controls aviation safety"

Actually, their role is to control safety relating to an individual aircraft and its passengers. They do not, on their own admission, control the societal risk to the public underneath the aircraft. That is a very different calculation.

Myth #12 – "Heathrow is effectively full"

No, it is not. This phrase has been used by the UK airport and airline industry for decades. It does not stop the continuing expansion of Heathrow. It was used as an argument for Terminal 4 and for Terminal 5 and it is now being used as an argument for another runway.

The industry argument to the Terminal 5 inquiry was that the operation of larger aircraft would satisfy the need for expansion without the need for a third runway.

Terminal 5 was only opened a few years ago and has massive unused capacity. The larger aircraft for which it was designed and configured have only just started to come on-stream. Despite this extensive, unused future capacity, the industry has tried to persuade the Government that a third runway is necessary, even before Terminal 5 is fully utilised. There is no shortage of capacity for the continual rise in passenger numbers in the interim before a new hub is built elsewhere.

If Heathrow really were full, the remedy is simple: for pricing to be increased to reduce demand. A recent press release by Heathrow Airport Ltd, Times, 17th April 2014, p 46, indicated that prices would be raised if a third runway was not approved. This is exactly what needs to happen at Heathrow to reduce the amount of traffic and the consequent harm.

Myth #13 – "Heathrow is the world's busiest international airport"

Heathrow airport operators have used this tired phrase for decades, somehow believing that this indicates how clever the company is to make it the busiest airport in the world. To passengers and residents of Greater London, it has merely indicated acute mismanagement and the reason for the decades of problems and increasing risks that passengers and residents have had to suffer.

Now it appears that this phrase is no longer true. It is an appropriate time for the pressure to be forcibly taken off Heathrow to make it progressively less busy in order to reduce the risks and harm that the airport generates.

Myth #14 – "Heathrow has to compete with European airports"

This is another decades-old industry myth, founded on a complete illusion created by the industry. The plain fact is that people fly to where they want to go. If passengers want to fly to a meeting in Paris, say, why should they conceivably decide to fly to London instead of Paris?

If they are trying to "compete" for transfer passengers, then it is much better for the UK that the transfer passengers do not fly via Heathrow and instead use other European airports for transfers.

Chapter 10
Conclusion

10.1 Leadership needed

It is the role of leadership to show the way to transformation; and the real focus of transformation here is to look for a solution that will satisfy all needs, not just to continue to grow air transport in the same unsustainable way. It is not good leadership to continue to use the same old faulty assumptions, which merely compound the same old flawed decisions.

Probably the biggest problem with the UK air transport system is that there is no established body and forum to provide leadership in decision-making in the interests of all members of the public. The system seems to have been hijacked by a few civil servants who have quietly set a policy mandate for the growth of their department and the industry they facilitate. They have simply transposed this mandate to the Commission, seemingly regardless of the consequences, and excluded public influence and checks on decisions. A proper, permanent body and funding is urgently needed instead of different, ad hoc, flawed, temporary solutions every few years.

10.2 A new airport would remove public safety risks

The building of an Estuary airport would make it possible to satisfy the needs of the UK air transport industry into the long-term future with potentially zero adverse impact on UK residents from noise and societal risk. No other airport solution can provide such a beneficial outcome.

This is a possibility that nobody in the industry, in Government or in previous analysis by the Airports Commission seems to have truly understood, although the Airports Commission recognises that "the difference in the total scale of [noise] impacts could be transformational" (6.15) and that this "next step will mark a watershed in the UK's approach" (6.41).

Exactly. The reasons this makes sense are the same reasons, and motivation, for offshore airports being built in Hong Kong, Japan and other places around the world; they are the real motivation for making this transformational decision for the UK and the UK air travel industry at this point in history. Yet then the Commission surprisingly concludes that no proposal has "presented a sufficiently powerful case for it to be recommended..." (6.43).

10.3 A reduction in activity at Heathrow is needed

No authority appears to have considered the prospect of a reduction in the use of Heathrow, while still retaining it to serve the local needs of West London. The Airports Commission's Interim Report focuses only on the expansion of Heathrow or the closure of Heathrow. Those are not the only choices:

- Firstly, the choice of no action at Heathrow is a real option because growth will proceed anyway with more use of larger aircraft as planned with the development of Terminal 5 without the third runway, so a third runway is entirely unnecessary

- Secondly, although closure is a better option in order to reduce the current harm and risks caused by even current Heathrow operation, progressive reduction in activity is also a real option.

Taken together, the building of an Estuary airport and the reduction of traffic at Heathrow could transform the future of airports policy in the UK – or at least in the South East – to suit all needs into the long term, easily and effortlessly. A major reduction in air traffic at Heathrow could remove the majority of the over-flight of London.

It is time for radical change in the UK air transport system, which takes full and proper account of the risks and harm that the industry creates. The old options are no longer sustainable.

Yet it is quite outrageous that the Commission has imposed a heavily onerous “Appraisal Framework” (Jan 2014), which means that anybody with a proposal is obliged to provide extensive documentation to prove that it is a “credible” proposal. This appears to be a device to ensure that only proposals for existing airports will appear to be credible to the Commission or the Government, and new proposals (even assuming they can afford the necessary speculative expenditure) will be able to be dismissed as not credible. Like objectors demonstrating harm, proposers should be provided with public funds to demonstrate benefit for a feasibility proposal for a public airport.

It is time for new leadership decisions – but where are the leaders with the new thinking to make those decisions?

The Transport Safety Commission

Whilst this report was being produced, a Transport Safety Commission was established within PACTS: The Parliamentary Advisory Council on Transport Safety.

Over the many years of PACTS' existence, it has appeared to focus mainly on road safety, on the basis that the majority of deaths have occurred on the roads.

However, the establishment of a Transport Safety Commission, to examine all modes of UK Transport Safety, is most welcome – and long overdue. The PACTS Commission's first inquiry rightly raises the key question, which underpins this report:

Who is Responsible?

It will be interesting to see whether the PACTS Commission will be forensic enough in its inquiry, and willing enough, to plunge deeply enough into the institutional and corporate ravines where responsibility for societal health and safety risks lies hidden.

Unfortunately, the indications are, from PACTS, that its Commission's "…recommendations are expected to focus on institutional arrangements for road safety. The Commission will not assume that all is satisfactory in rail and air safety and may decide to inquire into these areas too."

One can but hope…

Chapter 11
Extracts from the Terminal 5 Inquiry Report

There is a tendency in UK Government decision-making for each appointed public inquiry or commission to come to the same old conclusions, usually driven by a government approach that "this is the way we have always done it", and "don't rock the boat" by trying to change things.

The author wonders whether the Commission has read the Inspector's report of the Terminal 5 Inquiry, which did, at least, lay out in detail the objectors' cases, even if he then, astonishingly, chose not to "rock the boat". Here are a few extracts relevant to this report:

Aircraft noise:

"There can be no doubt that aircraft using Heathrow cause substantial disturbance and annoyance over a very wide area"... "The very great increase in the number of aircraft has made the noise climate worse for many, particularly in the early morning"... "Indeed, I have come to the firm view that the proposed new terminal would cause substantial harm in noise terms". (Summary, 88).

"My conclusion on night noise, based on all the evidence before me, is that noise from aircraft landing in the early hours causes substantial disturbance over a wide area and this leads to significant annoyance." (34.4.48).

The LA_{eq} index used to measure noise climate "was the subject of severe criticism much of which I consider to be well-founded" (34.4.42). "More significantly, I believe it fails to give adequate weight to the number of aircraft movements". "Even the [Gov.] Department recognised the deficiencies of the LA_{eq} system" (34.4.43).

Public Safety

"Terminal 5 would also result in a significant increase in the risk to public safety when measured in terms of individual risk."... "The fact that more people would be exposed to a material risk represents a real and substantial objection to Terminal 5" (Summary, 93).

"Apart from individual risk, Terminal 5 would increase the risk of a major air crash involving many casualties on the ground which would raise questions about the future of Heathrow" (Summary, 94).

Author's Note: It must be noted that Terminal 5 was only completed in 2008 and that the resultant harm and risk, referred to above, has mainly yet to come.

No Third Runway

"I agree with BAA that the evidence placed before me demonstrates that a third main runway at Heathrow would have such severe and widespread impacts upon the environment as to be totally unacceptable" (Summary 98).

No Short-term expediency

"It was not the role of this inquiry to set out long-term aviation policies for the South East. I warmly welcome the Government's decision to bring forward such policies and hope that these would ensure that future decisions on major airport development are not influenced by short-term expedience" (Summary 99).

No further development of Heathrow

"In the context of the Government's review, it should be assumed that no further major development would take place at Heathrow after Terminal 5" (Summary 99).

i.e. **No further development at Heathrow!**

P.S. Any reader left with any doubts about the societal risk to London should examine Figure 5.1 (Page 141) of the Airports Commission's Interim Report of December 2013, as partially illustrated on the following page:

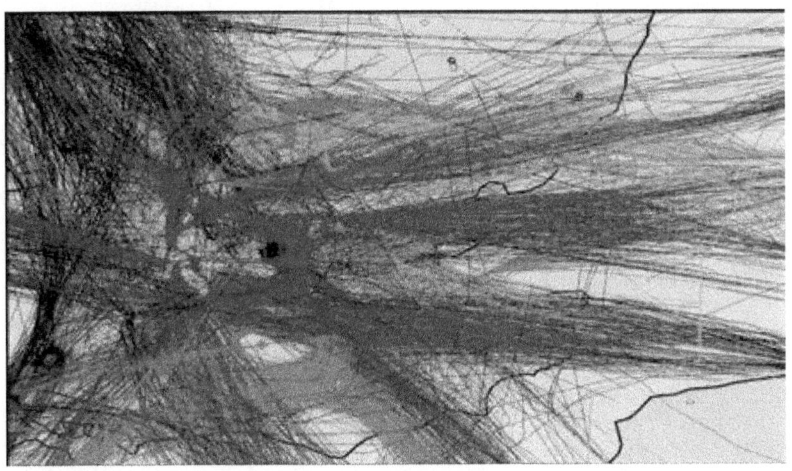

Figure 5.1: London airspace is highly complex and congested

From Airports Commission's Interim Report of December 2013. This figure contains public sector information licensed under the Open Government Licence v2.0.

Chapter 12
RECOMMENDATIONS

- Establish a UK Transport Safety Authority to be responsible for all individual and societal risks which might arise from UK transport operations

- Establish a UK Transport Health Authority to develop a more accurate and reliable noise measurement real-time mapping and control system together with analysis, research and prevention of the actual societal consequences which arise from transport noise exposure in people, animals and building structures

- Establish a UK Transport Authority as a permanent funded leadership body for public authority decision-making in relation to the development of the UK transport system

- These three leadership bodies to give free rights of access, contribution and discussion for members of the general public to understand and challenge the assumptions upon which decisions are to be made and the processes by which decisions are to be made

- In view of the statutory legal bar to access to the courts, to set up a formal system for appeal and resolution for members of the public placed at risk from air transport operations

- Begin the progressive reduction of activity at Heathrow; to reduce Heathrow's status from the busiest international airport in the world, to the Glidewell Inquiry level of 275,000 air traffic movements per annum, which will enable the societal risks to be substantially reduced

- Begin a decision-making process, with proper public and professional involvement, on whether an airport hub elsewhere is necessary for the UK

- Establish Whistleblower legislation and resources to safeguard those with concerns about corporate activities that may raise societal risks in any form to be able to express those concerns and be protected from repressive counter action

- No third runway and no further development at Heathrow!

www.ingramcontent.com/pod-product-compliance
Lightning Source LLC
Chambersburg PA
CBHW071004040426
42443CB00007B/659

* 9 7 8 1 9 1 0 2 6 8 0 1 8 *